THE
PURPOSE
Project

A PROCESS AND
JOURNAL TO DESTINY

Charmaine
COOPER

The Purpose Project
Copyright © 2021 by Charmaine R. Cooper

All rights reserved. No part of this publication
may be reproduced, distributed, or transmitted
in any form or by any means, including
photocopying, recording, or other electronic
or mechanical methods, without the prior
written permission of the author, except
in the case of brief quotations embodied
in critical reviews and certain other non-
commercial uses permitted by copyright law.

Tellwell Talent
www.tellwell.ca

ISBN
978-0-2288-3934-7 (Hardcover)
978-0-2288-3933-0 (Paperback)
978-0-2288-3935-4 (Ebook)

TABLE OF CONTENTS

Dedication v
Foreward vii
Endorsement xi
Endorsement xiii
About the Author xix
Introduction xxi

Chapter 1 Project You 1
Chapter 2 Do Your Research 11
Chapter 3 Assemble the Pieces 27
Chapter 4 Shut Out the Distractions 39
Chapter 5 Ride Your Wave 53
Chapter 6 Review and Refine 67
Chapter 7 Embrace Your Purpose 81
Chapter 8 Submit Your Purpose Project 95
Chapter 9 Re-Connect to Rest 109

Conclusion 119
Resources 121

DEDICATION

Dedicated to the memory of my Mother, Lurline A. Cooper, a strong, loving, black Business Woman. Although she left this earth far too soon, her life and legacy continue in me. I love you Mom.

Special thanks to my mentors and pastors; Roger Gushway and Maxine Gushway, who have believed in me, supported me and blazed a trail for me from the start. Your worth in my life is beyond description.

FOREWARD

Having known Charmaine Cooper for the past twenty-six years as her pastor and now humbly as a mentor and Spiritual Leader it gives me great honour to write a forward for this book.

I can assure you that the truths presented here were not from reading a book. They are truths that have been proven by living and practising them in her daily life.

Charmaine has made a tremendous contribution to multiple communities in this book. In *The Purpose Project* you will learn that you are made with, from and for PURPOSE. You will also receive sound advice as to how to unblock the hinderances that keep you from fulfilling your calling.

The truths and principles presented here will empower you to assemble the pieces, ride your wave, embrace your project and fulfill your purpose.

Charmaine's love for God, people and life is masterfully crafted and articulated through the following pages.

The concept that our life has purpose and it's a project that we must give attention to is a resonating theme captured throughout each chapter.

Charmaine unpacks the fact that by not taking the time to give attention to our purpose which is given by our Creator (God,) we are left incomplete. Too many of us have left this life project on the sidelines causing us to "Look through a lens of the past ....with a surge of regret."

She helps you, the reader to see your intrinsic value and the worth in launching out on the adventure of lifetime.

I appreciate the flow of her book by presenting many personal stories. You will especially enjoy hearing about her dog "Smokey". (*Not really a spoiler alert...*)

The Purpose Project gives you practical tools you can use to move you from the sidelines to re-engaging and having a fulfilled life.

You will be encouraged to birth change at the end of each chapter by answering thought provoking questions and journaling. I cannot say enough how important it is to answer these questions. They are there to serve you in this journey.

I can truly say the message chiseled out and articulated in this captivating read is a book whose time has come.

Kingdom blessing upon you my daughter Charmaine for taking the time and effort to pen these practical truths for others to engage with. As a result, many lives will be blessed and move forward into their journeys towards fulfilling the purpose of their lives. Rule and Reign (Rom 5:1).

Roger A.H. Gushway, Apostle/Founder of Kingdom Gate Equipping Centre, Toronto, Ontario

ENDORSEMENT

*C*harmaine addresses a vitally important topic—how do we get stuff done? More importantly she helps us identify the stuff that needs to get done. The most important project? Me, you, all of us--we are the project! With the Bible as her guide, she walks us through the project management process addressing the key steps in the journey: purpose, identity, passion, pacing, commitment, and perhaps a surprising step for some of us, rest. Each chapter has some probing questions and space to journal our thoughts. This is a very readable guide to help us with our most important project—the project of becoming who we are meant to be.

Dr. Michael Krause, R. J. Bernardo Family Chair of Leadership, Tyndale Seminary, Toronto ON

ENDORSEMENT

As I pour through the pages of my fresh copy of *The Purpose Project*, I see with teary eyes that my dear friend Charmaine Cooper has written a book on a topic that she is an authority on. Every turn of the page charms me, has me pulling my highlighter out with pure joy. The words are like transcriptions from above.

This book was written as a thoughtful interactive journal to help you lead your own charge into the life that you are intended to live. This book will become your self-written guide to the destiny that you were born for. The destiny that you long for and the destiny you must finally step into realizing in this life, and I can think of no other person than Charmaine to help you do just that.

I find divinity is often found in the assignments that we perform in service to others. We think we are doing something for someone, but really, they are doing something for us. That is what reading *The*

Purpose Project was for me. When we say 'yes' to helping someone that 'yes' reveals to us the real purpose of that project in our lives as we perform them. We get quiet in the doing. When we really listen to that inner heartbeat, we can ask unearthing questions like; Why am I here? Why am I doing this? Is this really helping? Do I serve a purpose? How can I live a life of meaning?

Then it happens like it happened for me...

You read the words in this book to get a little bit closer to the answer. You take an honest look at the 'project' called 'you' and finally realize this might be the best project of all time. This book makes you realize this. Although there is little we can control in this life- your life consists of many mini micro moments and decisions. Who we are, how we activate in the world and how we might see all things with love are some daily tools we can use in activating ourselves each day to truly understanding our purpose.

Stopping and looking inside at the stuff we do not want to see will get us where we need to go. We have all heard this, but Charmaine acts as the light source and our flashlight guiding us through the fear we have. Through our darkness and into a new light we can finally see who we really are and what our purpose is. This all may sound triggering but in Chapter five Charmaine simply and eloquently states, *"Triggers also are signals that the fear is left unaddressed."*

Fear no more- you are holding The Purpose Project in your hands and you are in good hands. I always think of one of my favorite Rumi quotes when I feel fear creeping in:

"Live life as if everything is rigged in your favor."

And the truth is—it is!! This quote makes me laugh! What are we scared of? Why is the truth so hard for us to see? Who we are, what we do, whom we meet and where we end up are all a part of the divine puzzle in place to see our purpose and there are no spare pieces. Charmaine says simply:

"Your purpose is right there in the healing process with you. Right in the fire. It is waiting for you to embrace it back."

Do what she says. Embrace yourself back. Use this journal and see yourself transform and trust me, you will.

Years ago, when Charmaine and I first met, many of the things I do today were not fully actualized in the world. Looking back through time I see that even then Charmaine could see in me all that I was, am and could be. She held me up, gave me support, opportunities and a stage to share my message. She does this for so many. She is a seer, supporter and transformer that has ears connected to *THE* source.

Today, she is sharing her message as a speaker, mentor, teacher, podcaster and thought-leader. Charmaine has stepped into a powerful facilitation position for others to learn from. As a woman of God, she helps anyone she meets, inspires or talks to, what she so eloquently shares in this book. She practices what she preaches and with a full heart she wishes everyone to live the most glorious life they can imagine.

When I look up the word purpose there are many alternate words for this kind of project: The ambition, desire, direction, wish, mission, idea, goal, and determination project. All of these words suit the chapters that Charmaine has effortlessly written to skillfully and inspirationally set you on your journey to self-discovery.

I have so many lines in this book circled that I could give it all away up front in this forward. But I have to share something she simply stated in Chapter one that I love:

"Everybody's obsessed with becoming what they want, but no one is paying attention to who they are. I have been there."

I love how real she is. But I could not agree with her more. Anything I have ever done that I feel most proud of is because it resonated with the truest sense of who I am and why I intrinsically feel I am here. Remember who you are and stop at nothing until you feel it. It doesn't have to look like anything; it needs to feel like everything.

Treat this book like your best friend wrote it for you. Cherish it. Reference it. Keep it close and read it over and over as you transform-and you will. The chapters are easily written so you can pick it up anytime and anywhere. The pages will leave you endlessly inspired to find your place in the cosmic web of the Universe to spread your message of service and love where you can.

I look forward to reading the many pages of her brilliance that will undoubtedly pour from her soul in additional books to come. May *The Purpose Project* inspire you to dig deeper inside yourself toward your inner phosphorescence that you are and may the instructions and advice help you unleash the unlimited potential in all you wish to do with your one precious life.

And to wrap this up I leave you one more time with Rumi:

"The Universe is not outside of you. Look inside yourself; everything that you want you already are."

I believe that. I believe in you and I believe in the power of Charmaine Cooper to guide you there.

With great love and joy I welcome you to your most beautiful journey yet,

Tiffany Pratt, Designer & Creative, Author and Speaker. love@tiffanypratt.com – Toronto, Ontario

ABOUT THE AUTHOR

Compassion, emotional presence and passion for the untold stories that shape our lives, are among the reasons why Charmaine stepped out to begin writing short books to propel and inspire people towards achieving their purpose.

Charmaine is a first generation Canadian, born and raised in the diverse, multi-cultural city of Toronto Ontario. As a single black woman Charmaine's twenty-three plus year career has spanned the education and public speaking sector within health and wellness. Having seen her fair share of challenges and struggle, there have been many opportunities to learn, grow, overcome and pay things forward. Coming from a long line up of empowered, independent and strong women, faith has been a huge factor within her heritage. Her Grandmother, Mother, Aunts and Grand Aunts all demonstrated courageous valour throughout challenging and testing times of their own lives. Although her pedigree is steeped with women who have made bold moves, Charmaine's journey of empowerment was a progressive one. Both internal and external factors were always present to try to discourage and cause her to shrink away from standing in her power of confidence.

In 2018, Charmaine commenced her pursuit in the completion of her Master's degree of Theology. While still holding speaking engagements of larger and intimate sizes, consulting health and wellness clients both online and in person, Charmaine continues to find joy in helping others to untap their inner wealth and purpose.

Charmaine is the Host of The Char Candid Podcast where she supports countless listeners through weekly episodes and interviews that inspire and provoke to higher perspective-oriented choices. She believes that growth and development will always consist of discomfort. It is a resolute mindset to continue in the midst of discomfort, however that is the staple to great achievements and fulfillment. That is both the beauty and irony of the great class room of life.

Charmaine Cooper IG: @charcoop2
Char Candid Podcast IG: @charcandidpod

INTRODUCTION

Sitting down and counting the costs is essential to laying down the realities associated with any new project. Often at times, when considered, the project is put off until a later time, if even done at all. However, if entered into with eyes wide open and hearts attentive, it is the most rewarding and developing process that one can experience.

I have sat down, over the years, to consider countless projects. Some, I've secretly entered into kicking and fighting. Other projects that I've started were met with not as much reluctance. But there was always the internal *sigh* that said; "Here we go. Are you ready for this?" Perhaps I'm not alone who has felt this. In fact, I have reason to believe that I am not.

Not all projects are created equally. But they all are taken on with a similar process. It's a process that we have all already become aware of, even proficient at. From grade school to the latter years of our lives. We have always had pending projects, big or small awaiting our commencement, attention or completion.

What about the project of purpose? Where are you at in the process of that project? Have you commenced? Have you given it attention or have you ignored it? What stage of that process are you at? Have you considered what it will cost to take this on? Have you considered what it has costed or will cost you to put it off? These are questions we must all ask ourselves.

You are more than a title, function or set of skills. You are housing the very real possibilities that were meant for you to do in this earth because of who you are on the inside. The true you. And the truth is, you are the only one who can make the decision to discover the beauties and the learnings of the project that is you! The Purpose project: You.

CHAPTER 1

Project You

Who doesn't love a good project? Whether it's a new garden, a renovated bathroom or school assignment, projects can offer a range of exhilarating as well as taxing feelings. Let's just dissect this for a moment, shall we? What does it actually take to execute a project from beginning to end?

All projects begin with a choice to start. Whether we want to or not, at some point there is a conscious decision to do it or a decision to ignore it. Do we walk by the unfinished rooms in our home hallways and simply pretend that there isn't a need for attention? Do we turn a blind eye to the cluttered closet. Has that spare empty nest bedroom become a storage room of junk and old furniture? What about the final research paper, the business idea or the leaking faucet? Every day we choose to either bypass or respond to the priority of projects.

If we choose to respond, from there, we start to research the various elements that it will require to haul off this project successfully. We count the costs. We investigate and do our research. Comparing vendors and suppliers. We look into the past to better understand what we are working with in order for a favourable outcome.

My mother was a research queen. As a child, I recall seeing the cut-out coupons on our kitchen and hallway table. She was always researching. She was always comparing. To behold the intensity with which she conducted this process of researching was a sight, when I paused enough to notice. She was relentless. And although many times, other priorities would arise like feeding her two small kids on a single parent income, she only put those projects on pause. I noticed that sooner or later, sometimes through tears and exhaustion, she would return to her research to re-launch those projects. Like my Mother, for us to stop at the research level would barely scratch the surface.

After the research is done, we need to assemble the components of the material discovered. Often at times this part doesn't make sense and seemingly looks like an assembly of pure chaos. Mixed and matched slivers of information. A mash-up of segments that each possess their own hidden genius but together, can leave us dumbfounded. If we are honest, the natural tendency, here is to quit, throw in the towel and leave the unassembled project right where we left it. But hold on! Let's keep going a bit further. It's at this very point where a different gear can kick in for us. If we choose to continue making sense of the mash-up we soon can discover that it is not by happenstance or by a mere whim that these pieces are before us. It is rather, by sheer providence that they lay before us. It is at this point where the treasure hunt challenge is met with determination! If we put aside distractions and lock into this project like a bull dog latched onto a bone, we could see a beautiful outcome. At first it can be gruelling but there is something fascinating that's taking place here. There's a newly found grace. A systematic groove. A rhythmic dance that is discovered and it's soon accompanied by a passion! And so, we enter not just an 'ebb and flow', but we enter our 'stride and flow'.

The amazing thing is, if we choose to stay in this momentum, we soon achieve a fulfilment at the close of the project that seemed only a far-off dream when we first started. We've all experienced what I've briefly described at some point or points in our lives. And what a journey!

Now, there are projects. And then there are PROJECTS! What would you say if I told you that the ultimate project that trumped every other project you could possibly start in this life was the project of You? Yes, YOU!

I've noticed that people aren't readily willing to take on this project. Mothers give their whole lives to their children and families, discarding themselves as a result. Teenagers get consumed in the distractions of measuring themselves against a false standard offered by social media and peers. Singletons become consumed with becoming attached, even if it is to the wrong person. And married couples daydream of being unattached, even if it's from the right person. Everybody's obsessed with becoming what they want. But no one is paying attention to who they are. I've been there.

We are more than a title. We are more than our present circumstances in societal life. We are more than what we've heard, what we've seen or even what we've been told. We literally are so much more.

How long will we walk by the hallways of our lives and ignore the unfinished rooms of who we are, and who we were created to be? You were created to be more than an ignored project of potential. We have all heard where the majority of potential ends up: In the graveyard, never untapped. Well let's change that. And let's start the change by looking at the truth that has always been there. Can I invite you to stop being consumed with the expectations, affirmations and attention from others for a moment and look at this a bit more deeply with me?

The truth is; you are the only one who can choose to break the cycle of ignorance. Ignorance is not bliss. Ignoring your purpose can lead to misusing your life. It actually is insulting, even abusive to your purpose. I want us to let that resound for a moment with us. It is abusive to YOUR purpose. So, let's take a deeper look at this beautiful, raw, complex yet brilliant project of YOU together! Let's go.

CHAPTER & JOURNAL REFLECTION:

1. What were some projects that you have avoided?

2. What were the reasons for your avoidance?

3. What was one project that you completed?

4. How did you feel at the conclusion of that project?

5. Do you, believe that you/your vision or dreams are worth attending to?

Journal your thoughts:

The Purpose Project

CHAPTER 2

Do Your Research

Sitting in the library of my University, after having received my syllabus description of my final research paper, I recall staring at a blank search window tab on my laptop. It's the feeling that I've come to know so well, as I pursue the completion of my Master's degree twenty years later in life! The same thoughts come to me every time. I need to navigate my way through the maze of overwhelming thoughts of discouragement and doubt that routinely come. Typically, after a silent prayer, the first step through that maze is always led by a strike of a key on my laptop into the search window. I tap into the online portal of my institutes library, *'et voila'*! The process has begun. I start to research the historical accounts, various references and authorities on the subject matter. This at first seems arduous and random but a slow rhythm begins to unfold. I follow the guideline set in my syllabus outline, and a start to leave no stone unturned. At the far back of my mind is the anchoring thought to "always have a reference to fall back on". To do that, I commit to studying, reading a wealth of topics in such a way that I can pinpoint the exact page and reference to support my theory/thesis and supportive arguments.

The definition of research is: *the diligent and systematic inquiry or investigation into a subject in order to discover or revise facts, theories, applications.* Every application and argument in order to stand must have a factual foundation in order for it to stand. I mean, how absurd would it be if I wrote a theoretical paper without solid grounds of reference?

Let's apply that to when we look at our own lives? So many times, we have come to conclusions, summaries, theories and arguments about ourselves without the due diligence of researching the facts. We come to believe our non-factually based conclusions and build entire lives upon them. Worse yet, we perpetuate that onto others around us and portray those conclusions as factual. And therefore, creating new points of reference for others about us. We even believe them about ourselves. And we all know that if we believe a lie long enough, it becomes our own, twisted truth.

Why not do the research? Yes, it may take more work and a bit more intestinal fortitude, but let's move from staring at the blank search screen of our lives and strike the first key!

Key strike #1: Who are you? Global studies on twins brought up separately from one another's birth have confirmed that people are more than a product of their environments. They are a product of their DNA strands. Twins, separated for years, sometimes decades were found to act the same. This astounding fact had confirmed for researchers that the DNA strands of twins had been responsible for giving them their tandem bents of behaviour, not their environments.

Let's apply that to our lives. We have all been brought up in various environments. Some much more difficult sometimes more destructive than others. Yet we have also learned of individuals who have flourished in life even after having been brought up in similar, if not more destructive environments. How is that possible? It is because intrinsically in every person there are DNA structures that determine bents towards success, betterment and achievement. In fact, these DNA determined bents are not limited to an ethnicity, gender, a particular generation or demographic. It is inclusive of all human beings. No matter which side of the track you were born on.

Do the research. Do you know how unlikely and difficult it is for a sperm to swim against a natural current in order to fertilize one egg of a woman? The journey of sperm from the male body to the female body is a multi-complex, risky and remarkable one. Out of the millions of sperm that a healthy male will produce only about 15% of sperm actually make their way towards the cervix of the woman to fertilize an egg.

Do you realize the dangers that a baby encounters in the womb at conception and through the birth canal? I'm certainly not an authority in conception and birth but I do know that the evidence indicates that there is purpose driving every step towards life and that first breath! You are more than a family name and ancestry. You are more than the circumstances that you were born into. You are an incredible force that has already made it through some of the most challenging and most constraining of circumstances. Your ancestry, your family, the natural birth processes were all used as vehicles to get you here, they do not determine the reason that you are here. The recognition of this force starts with your Creator. From there it's a beautifully woven discovery process for us to learn who we are: which is far more than what we possibly could imagine.

Key Strike #2: Why are you here? This is a part of the research that is critical to the heart of the research.

Without the "why" we lose focus for the "what". Too many people live their entire lives going from "what to what" and deal constantly with a drive of non-fulfillment or frustration. All because this part of the question is never fully understood. Perhaps, it has never even been asked. Without the knowledge of the purpose of a product, that product is subject to abuse. A screw driver is a poor supplement for a hammer, whether it can hit a nail or not. The mastery of that screw driver is only found in its connectivity to a fitted nail head. A car is a poor supplement for storage of old household items and boxes. Although you can pack items safely in the trunk, backseat and front seat, it's mastery is only realized when a driver starts the ignition and moves it out of park, onto the road. Understanding why we exist is rudimentary to living non-abusive lives. By "non-abusive", I mean, allowing our mastery to be developed and realized. This doesn't come right away. However, there are signs along the way, hints and clues from early in life that can help to affirm these truths.

Not always, but often these clues were always before our eyes. Brilliant culinary artists can often track early hints to their mastery as children. Prima ballerinas often were found to constantly be spinning or dancing as toddlers and young children. Successful entrepreneurs, often can recall constantly being frustrated in Monday's 9-5 work. Some, even found it challenging to hold onto a job as teens or young adults. Others, were possibly the children that always wanted to get creative in how they earned allowance or independent funds for that activity they wanted to do.

The point here is, the clues can be tracked. Why is that? Could it be because you are supposed to discover why you have the bent that you have? Could it be less of a mystery than many of us make it out to be? Someone, who I believe to be God, is not trying to keep this discovery from you, but rather keep it for you!

Key strike #3: How are you to live out your purpose? There really is only one solution to this vast and extensive question. That is, to consult with the purpose-manual.

When you order a new device online or purchase a new piece of equipment from a department store, the first thing you do is to search for the user's manual. Not everyone does this, I know. I have personally been guilty of bypassing the user's guide out of sheer zeal and excitement, even arrogance at times to put the item together myself. Needless to say, the outcome was miserable, lopsided or even malfunctioning. We all know how asinine, even arrogant it is for any consumer to order an item that they are not an expert on and not consult with the manufacturer's recommendation for that product.

If that is the case with common merchandise, why should it be any different when it comes to understanding the use and purpose of the most incredible item ever manufactured: Human lives?

The manufacturer's guide is not the opinions of others. It is not the environment that we are in or came from. It is not even what we think best at times based on our own experiences at various stages and phases of our lives. The manufacturer's guide to humanity is not found in a textbook or scientific study manual. They are only surface explanatory literature to the finite composites of who we are. Yes, they are inspiring on their own; which has given birth to the brilliance of medical science and biology. But they of themselves cannot offer the guide to a comprehensive understanding to matters of the heart, dreams and the inner spirit of a man. That can only come from one manufacturer's book. Your grandmother might have referred to it as the "good book". You might have ignored it most of your life. But it is the sole heart revealing, soul inspiring, purpose finding guide that has existed since the beginning of time. It is the Bible.

When conducting sound research, anthropology researchers often excavate the earliest sources of evidence and artifacts. The first signs of civilization and even literature reveal so much of the centuries long gone. Their research helps us to better understand civilization today. The earliest and most accurate sources to humanity can only be found at the beginning of time. And the evidence has been captured for us by God's design, using the inspired hearts of men and women who have lived out, and penned down these God thoughts and facts.

What are the God thoughts and facts about you? Do you even believe that God cares to think about you? I'm here to tell you emphatically, that He does! And your purpose, our purposes existed from the beginning of time. Before you and I even entered into this world, we were in the heart and plan of the Creator. Thoughts and plans for us and our ancestors that are so vast while at the same time so much more intimate than you could imagine. These thoughts are good.

You are not here by mistake. You are not here without a purpose. You are not here to merely exist and occupy space until you expire. You are here for good. Not because of the things you can do. It's deeper than that. It is rather, because the manufacturer has already called you good and placed His seal of approval already on you. No product can be passed for distribution until it has passed inspection at the production level. If it's in the stores or online, it is because it had to have passed the inspection. So great news! Even before we made our first mistake of many mistakes in our lives, we already passed inspection. How do I know that? Simple. Because you made it to this earth!

And so, someone believed in us enough to bring us to this world. Someone already approved us. Even if others have disapproved us our whole lives. We are approved, even if we disapproved ourselves. The only way to grasp the understanding of how to accomplish your purpose is to embrace your purpose given through the manual for your life. Not a book of rules and religious rituals. But a book of love, assistance and relationship.

We cannot help but relate to the classic 1883 Italian children's tale of Pinocchio by Carlo Collodi. A story of a naughty wooden puppet who disobeyed his father's instructions and rebelled just like a little boy would. He persisted in his selfish behaviour in spite of Geppetto, the puppet maker and his loving father's corrections offered. It was not until Pinocchio finally realized that to truly become the little boy he so desired to be, he had to embrace his purpose. That purpose was not to live a life of selfishness but to be open to leading a life with his heart and compassion towards others. I've always loved a great children's tale, long into my adulthood. Often at times, the unearthed treasures of these tales transcend the understanding of little children and speaks loudly to the children who we all still are on the inside, well into our adulthood. The message of Pinocchio still speaks to generations today. Why is that? It is because, whether you believe in God or not, you know you didn't choose to come here yourself. Yet, here we all are. And many of us started the journey of trying to make things happen for ourselves, sometimes at any cost. And many of us are still trying to run from, even ignore the possibility of their own Geppetto, their maker. It is not until we recognize that our Geppetto (Creator) is not trying to manipulate or control our lives that we can experience true liberty. Our Creator is not here to force us to do anything. He only desires a true and voluntary Father/son, Father/daughter relationship.

CHAPTER & JOURNAL REFLECTION:

1. Who do you believe that you are?

2. Why do you believe that you are here?

3. Do you feel that you have been true to your purpose?

4. How have you been living out your purpose?

5. Has the method that you have employed feel right and true to what is on the inside of you?

6. Do you feel that your mistakes have influenced or affected you living out your purpose?

Journal your thoughts here:

The Purpose Project

The Purpose Project

CHAPTER 3

Assemble the Pieces

Life happens. This is a phrase that we have heard for the majority of our lives. It often reflects the short end of the stick perspective that we have either embraced or resolved to fight. As some would put it; it's the 'do-do' that hits the fan in life's circumstances, and the associated disappointments that we experience along the way. There isn't a sole person past, present or future who will not at some point in their lives have to ascertain and take stock of the pieces of their lives. Life is happening all around us.

Yesterday, I visited a dear friend of mine, who has been raising her nine-year-old son completely on her own since his birth. This little boy as far as I can recall has had an incredibly brilliant mind and empathetic heart. One day while on a road trip somewhere with her, her four-and-a-half-year-old son, who was in the back seat at the time said something that shocked me. He said "Auntie Charmaine, your mother loved you very much and is very proud of you". He had no idea that my mother had died over 18 years earlier and that she was a single mother who I loved tremendously and was my best friend. He had no idea that that week in particular (around her birthday) I was missing her deeply. His mother never spoke to him about my relationship to my mother or anything. All I know is that his words touched me to the depths of my heart and tears filled my eyes with gratitude for this divinely sent message through this little boy. It was literally as if he possessed a sixth sense. I know that it was God sending a personalized message to me through this little, beautiful boy.

And so, while visiting their home recently, I saw a huge puzzle that spanned their entire dining room table. As I approached the table, I saw that most of the pieces were all still separated but turned right side up in order to see the images. I said, "Oh! You're putting a puzzle together!" To be honest, it looked intimidating. But I said it with an optimistic tone and smile. My friend answered back and said, "Yes, we are. It's our second time, however, assembling it. We already completed the puzzle before". She said it with such a contentment for the process, in spite however tedious it may have appeared to me. I was fascinated. I gazed at it a bit longer, as she spoke from across the hall in her kitchen. The observation I made did not hit me until many hours later, while I was back at home.

As I reflected on the puzzle, I thought of how many times I had had the perfect picture of my life, broken up into small pieces? So much to the point of not being able to even recognize the image anymore. How many of us all have been there? How often have we had to assemble the pieces slowly and strategically which takes time and attention to only have it be dissembled again, and the process started over?

By the age of twelve, I knew what I wanted my entire life to look like. I had it planned through my wedding, out to the birth of my last child at the age of thirty-one. The white picket fence with the handsome architect husband were distinct parts of the story that gelled just right and followed their cue flawlessly. My picturesque life was radiating from my table of life's aspirations. Losing my mother to cancer at an early age and losing my dad at an even earlier age to absenteeism was not a part of that picture.

Not finishing my university degree due to my own neglect and then my unresolved trauma was also not a part of that dream. My puzzle pieces were left disassembled, and they remained untouched for years. As I passed through the hallways of my life I would at times glance over at the table of dreams, and I accepted the reality of the hopeless disappointment.

Until one day, when I started to approach the table of dreams again with bravery. I commenced the reassembling process. It was surreal to look at the enormity or task ahead of me. But with the help from my manufacturer, I committed to trusting the process of healing by acknowledging what I had ignored for so long.

The pieces of our dreams, aspirations and lives don't always come together or stay together the way we had originally hoped. But the brilliant part is that if we would be brave enough, even vulnerable enough to acknowledge the pain, the regret and the hurt, the healing can start to enter the wounds of our lives. What can happen subsequently is nothing short of amazing!

A new rhythm, a new stride, a new momentum emerges from within us. And before we know it, a new picture appears. A picture of hope instead of despair. Forgiveness instead of bitterness. Fulfillment instead of emptiness. Laughter instead of sorrow. The potential of these new dreams and images lay unrealized every day we choose to ignore the pieces on the table of our lives. I recall an analogy that a great leader once shared in a conference that I attended. He said, "Though the individual ingredients of a cake are often bitter on their own, when blended and tried in the fire together, what comes out is a beautiful creation."

Don't focus on looking at the individual pieces of your life. But like a master puzzle assembler, take a step back sometimes from the table for an aerial view. See the bigger picture. See the purpose in the individual ingredients. And embrace the process of reassembling the pieces. Like my friend, the process of assembling the pieces may be multiple. But each time you are courageous enough to do it, a newer, fresher image can emerge.

It's not a race. Master puzzlers, often take time and embrace the extended process as an enriching one. Sometimes, walking away from the puzzle pieces and returning at a later date or time with fresher eyes has renewed vigour. It's ok to walk away at the point of frustration. When we grow tired and things get overwhelming, it's ok to step away. It's good. It's humane, even.

When I was ready to address the section of my life with my absentee father, it had taken me over eighteen years. I started the process in my early twenties and was met with rejection after rejection. I was puzzled as to why a loving father who I knew as a child, found it impossible to love me as a young adult, after years of absenteeism. I was looking too closely to the puzzle pieces. I had individual pieces in my hands of rejection, sadness and personal abandonment. It wasn't until I stepped back and saw the bigger picture of his hurt, and his childhood pain, and his sense of personal childhood rejection that was triggered as an adult, did I begin to understand. I started to see and understand more.

Addressing the aspect of my own neglect, resulting in the incompletion of my post-secondary formal learning, took me twenty years to look at with sincerity. The feeling of it being too late for me to achieve anything was only the intense glare at the same puzzle pieces over and over in my mind's eye. Puzzle pieces of failure, embarrassment, neglect and deserved punishment. I was too close to the puzzle. I had to first come to terms with that. I had to realize that although I was responsible for the actions of my past, I was also responsible for the actions that created my future. There are various aspects that I am still working on and I don't advise anyone to take my extended period of removal of formal study as a template suggestion. If I'm honest, some of the areas, I prolonged, unnecessarily. However, time turned out to be faithful teacher. It revealed for me the currents of fear of success that threatened every academic or business endeavour that I had. I faced these realities by first approaching the table from a different perspective. I sat down with intentionality. I looked at other sections of the puzzle. I started to see past pieces of my life that led me to believe those lies. A guidance/career councillor who expressed his disagreement with me on my career choice held a greater rank in my lack of confidence than he should have. For some reason, I allowed a perfect stranger with the title of councillor to guide me in fear and doubt in my own ability. Perhaps, the absence of my father at the time had much more to do with that, then I realized. The point is, being too close to the disassembled pieces, would not have allowed me to see that. I had to consider more than my present pieces. I had to take stock of more than my current experience.

Have you taken stock of your choices based on previous experiences? Have you intently with courage to the pieces? If you choose to do so, please remember that as you do so, you're certainly not doing it alone. You have never been left in this life experience alone. Even if you felt as if you were for the majority of it. It took feats of faith for you to even make it into this life. It will take feats of faith to carry you through it. Feelings often contradict the truth of faith. And the truth of faith often cannot be grasped by facts or feelings. This is a natural tension in any project of destiny and purpose. There arises torrents of doubt and fear in the light of faith and hope. The truth is, in the midst of ever internal storm, God was and always will be with you. He is there to help make sense of and assemble your pieces.

CHAPTER & JOURNAL REFLECTION:

1. What are some of the plans that you had that did not work out?

2. Did those fallen through plans impact you? If so, how?

3. What are the individual pieces of your life that are hard to look beyond?

4. Have you seen, are you willing to see a bigger picture beyond individual disappointments? If so, what is the bigger picture?

5. What do you believe could be the upside to walking away from broken pieces for a while and coming back to them later on?

Journal your thoughts here:

The Purpose Project

Charmaine R. Cooper

CHAPTER 4

Shut Out the Distractions

It seemed as though every time I started to pursue a relationship or a love interest, my other pursuits in life were placed on hold. Then, to my amazement, when the pursuit of that particular relationship was placed on hold, the other areas of my life accelerated, even began to bloom again. This baffled me for some time. I didn't understand it. Perhaps I even resented it a bit, if I were to be honest. In hind-sight, those relationships were not the right ones for me and eventually the realization that either I was not the right person for them or they were not the right person for me became clear. Yet, at the time these relationships were nice distractions that contributed to me feeling good. They offered me a light and pleasant distraction of attention. A part of me enjoyed the relaxed attentiveness to my goals and disciplinarian practices. I enjoyed the attention and giving of attention to another person in order to receive more attention from that person. Whether it was in one particular relationship dynamic or if it was from one relationship to another, there was a perpetual pull to slide into the bliss of distraction. Is it possible for distraction to become a blissful state? I think all we would need to do, to truly ascertain the answer to that question is to look around us and the inattention that we have been primed to embrace today. Social media and the various other playgrounds of life vie for our attention. The appeal lies within the deception of ease and fun. Like a shiny new object, distractions call to us from afar usually when purpose and progress us at the forefront of my thoughts. But it's not vying for our attention. We must learn to see it for what it is: It is vying for our purpose and destiny. It is the pull to keep you from realizing the treasure in walking out your purpose. And although it may seem like it is just a mild, innocent and harmless distraction, it can kill purpose. Slowly. This cycle became my reality at various important junctures of my life; my schooling, my faith, promotions within my career and business pursuits. With every step forward there seemed to be a desire for me to pause a bit and dance with a distracting pursuit for a moment. They were moments that relieved the sense of responsibility. They were moments that relieved the tension between discipline and play. They were moments that stagnated me and often left me in a microcosm all its own that eventually required all too much of my energy. It finally dawned on me that I was the only one who could realize and break this cycle for myself. I either committed to the purpose project or I committed to a foreign project. Both would take the same degree of energy. Both would require the same amount of time. But both would not yield me the same results. I had a choice. We all have these choices.

Why do cycles of distraction lure us into the bliss of carelessness and inattention? Why are they so appealing to us in times of great momentum and progress? These are hard questions that I asked myself. These are far too frequent realities for us not to ask. We live in a society that praises living for the weekend. And in so doing, communicates a message to us that the weekdays of our lives are arduous, hopeless and lifeless. We have all believed or lived this out to some degree, but the question is, "why do we believe this"? Is there no purpose to our Monday to Fridays of life? Is there no thrill that can be discovered? Are all the routine disciplines and structured practices in our lives absent of enjoyment? Many, would say "yes". However, upon a closer look, a heart-revealing look, we could see something more.

Take for instance the final paper assignment that we had to complete in school. What if, you studied a subject that excited you immensely?

Whether it bored others or not, was irrelevant. It thrilled you! You owned your role in unearthing some new discoveries of that particular topic for yourself and/or for your Professor. You embraced the growth and the insights that you gained on the specificity of the topic. You found the lesson. You found the treasure. You became a benefactor of the discovery process. After having invested yourself, you were able to divest yourself in your research paper and showcase that to others. By sheer diligence, you became the expert on that topic. Perhaps to your professor. Perhaps to the class or even a larger audience. In this scenario, the paper would become less of an arduous task and more of a passion. The paper would possess a greater value. One that is worth the attention and shutting out of all other distractions.

Ok, herein lies the application we can take and apply to our lives. This is the untapped truth of every juncture we take: YOU are the worthwhile topic that is deserving of the attention through self-discipline and the shutting out of distractions.

For me, the distractions happened to be misfit relationships. But it can be completely different for many people. Whatever it is for you, chances are you already know it well. It's brilliance appeals to you, only when you take your eyes off the prize and find yourself sitting in an abyss of purposelessness. But when you understand who you are, and why you are here, it is impossible for purposelessness to exist even in the minutest of detailed life.

So, in order to successfully shut out distractions, begin by seeing your life as a purpose oriented one on every scale. Work, home, personally and professionally; see your life from a purposeful perspective. You are filled with destiny. You therefore, can bring it to your job, share it at home, and you can divest it in your dreams and goals.

Secondly, choose to not believe the lie of the new, shiny, bright object vying for your attention. From a shopping spree or a new car to vegging out in front of the big screen from your couch for hours on end. The promise that the distraction gives is empty and often at times short lived. Especially when it calls for you to shut down a purpose-oriented project or discipline. Now, I am not saying that there is no time for leisure, enjoyment and play. We all need to balance our lives and make room for people who positively contribute to our lives and who we can contribute to in return. What I am saying is that you can embrace enjoyment in your disciplines only when you see them correctly. This takes effort to do. It should be done with intentionality.

Thirdly set boundaries that safe guard your choice to not believe the lies of distraction. Your boundaries can look like a time frame that is dedicated solely to the project or goal, where this timeline is exclusively devoted to the goal. Maintaining a pattern for that timeline is also very useful in respecting that boundary. For example: reading every morning for one hour. Or writing/composing every day for a number of hours at a specific time of day. Routine for your disciplines promote momentum. Routine for your discipline also respects your objective and increases its worth. Never see boundary setting as constricting, but rather see it as freeing.

Fourthly, offer yourself opportunity to see a fresh perspective of your project, goal and vision. That may look like you bouncing your thoughts to a trusted friend, partner or mentor. Being open to feedback along the way is beneficial because a trusted voice can be a voice of encouragement while serving as a guard rail reminder. Guard rails help to keep a moving vehicle in the lane and on track to where it should be going. Guard rails also help to guide our vision in front, where it belongs, rather than to the peripheral scenery on either side of a moving vehicle. These trusted and proven voices in your life can serve to keep you accountable to the origin of your goal and project. They can serve to keep you in your mode of momentum, by encouraging forward momentum. At the same time, these voices can point out things that you of yourself may have not seen or considered.

One of my dear mentors gave me an illustration years ago that has stuck with me ever since. She said to watch out for the 'blind spot syndrome'. A blind spot can harm you, your vision and dream if you are not careful. It is not what you know about yourself that others know about you that harms you. It is not even what you know about yourself that no one else knows about you that harms you. But it is, rather, what you don't know about yourself that others know and see about you that harms you. These are the blind-spots that if left unchecked can shipwreck or collide our lives with things they were not supposed to collide with. Mentorship is a gem and an invaluable perspective that many people take for granted. Mentorship can assist you in seeing from a broader, yet more detailed perspective all at the same time. The hallmark of mentorship is trust. To give someone the right and authority to speak into your life, means that you trust them and believe that they have your good outcome at the heart of their mentorship. It also means that you have granted someone permission to speak harsh truths to you, when needed. Some truths that you may not want to hear. But at the end of the day, you believe in that voice of reason. And you trust that voice.

Mentorship not only is anchored in trust, but it is marked by respect and honour. Why is respecting and honouring mentorship so crucial to shutting out distractions? Every great student, athlete, artist, had a great mentor at some stage of their discipline. Whether the mentor is known to the public or not, the place and worth of that mentor in the eyes of the protege doesn't change. The great Michael Jordan had a Coach who he respected as his mentor to the point that in one of his last Championship games with the Bulls, he refused to play unless that Coach coached the team. The late great Gregory Hines who was an accomplished tap-dancer had the honour of having the incomparable, late, great Sammy Davis Junior as mentor, friend and dance partner. The desire to honour and respect those before you, who have poured a great deal into your life is a driving force to wanting to give back in a way that would make them proud. It causes you to devote yourself to sharpening your talent and skillset. Mentorship does not cause you to lose your identity, but it is a means that allows you to discover your identity and become what you were purposed to be.

CHAPTER & JOURNAL REFLECTION:

1. What is your honest relationship with distractions? Do you welcome them or resist them?

2. Can you trace back to a time when you had great momentum and became sidetracked by a distraction?

3. What were some of the elements of attraction to the distraction?

4. Did any of the parts of the project suffer by attending to the distraction? What part of the project suffered?

5. What are some of the safeguards to distraction? Can you or have you implemented any of them?

Journal your thoughts here:

The Purpose Project

CHAPTER 5

Ride Your Wave

Waves intimidate some people and exhilarate others. To witness this fascinating reality, all we have to do is look at the ocean shores known for their reputations of great wave sizes and observe those who are taking them on and those who are at the shoreside looking on. From the safety of the shore, people gasp, cheerlead, judge, and sometimes criticize. But what is never done from the shoreside is 'riding the wave'. Have you ever thought of what surfers are doing while they are riding the wave? I've never surfed myself, but I can imagine that their focus is not on the individuals at the shoreside. Especially in the cases of monstrous waves that they are approaching or in the process of riding. Why is that? It is likely because at that very time, to shift their focus onto those shoreside spectators would compromise and threaten the very continuity of their momentum. Isn't it interesting that those who are making no momentum and taking no risk have much to say about those who are? Those on the waves of momentum, say very little about those on the shoreside because they are keenly aware of the danger it poses to their momentum, even their own safety.

We can learn much from our surfing school masters. The waves of life, goals and projects can seem daunting at times, especially at the beginning. It takes finding your proper footing. It takes trust in who you have become through your experience and process of surfing. It requires the tandem partnership of farsightedness and near sightedness of the surfer. It also requires sensitivity to timing.

Momentum comes to every purpose-oriented venture of life. No matter how long it may seem to be building, know that it is building. A surfer may catch a wave that seems as if it will be of enormous proportions to only end up being small. Regardless of the outcome, it was a wave. With each repeated effort, his/her confidence and expectation continues to rise.

Shouldn't it be the same in purpose-oriented ventures? Just because you have stepped out into a venture, but you have yet to step into your stride or your flow, doesn't mean that you are to give up. The truth is, we cannot determine the size of our waves on mere circumstantial appearances. If we focus on what we know to do; our disciplinarian practices, our learnings and our diligent attention to details, the wave will come in due time. When we focus on the skill, the momentum will come. Ask any athlete. It's when you focus only on the momentum and discard the skill that things fizzle out or worse yet, we risk the life of our goal altogether.

There exists today in our society another element of momentum that we must address. That is; the fear of momentum. When you first sit down in the seat of a roller coaster car, what is that feeling that fills your stomach? What comes over you and permeates your being? Excitement and nervousness! No matter what side of the coin of emotion you find yourself interpreting that feeling on, it's still the same energy! Fight or flight comes from a surge of adrenaline that is in direct response to your interpretation of a circumstance. Notice, for a moment, the telling variety of faces of roller coaster riders. If you look on their faces of those who first sit down, you would see smiles, hear nervous giggles, observe blank fearful stares, hear words of regret or complete silence! The point is, everyone sitting in that seat, having been buckled-in and strapped-down is now counting the cost and navigating through the torrents of emotions. They are mapping out the racing possibilities in their mind of what could and will be. Once the movement of the cars starts off slowly, what we have all heard next is revealing of our humanity. These words have undoubtedly been shuttered or shouted; "No! Stop the car! Let me off"! But by then, of course it is normally too late. Why the outburst? Why the outcry of regret? I believe one answer to that is the 'fear of momentum'!

As that car starts its way up the steep journey to the top of the first drop, anything and everything can flood through the minds of people. To the fearful, it is the dread of the momentum and where it might lead them. Will they be able to bare the pit-less feeling in their stomach? Will their heart or lungs be able to overcome? Will they die? The fear of momentous speed or accelerated movement has always tempted the fearful to feel completely out of control and fearful of death. Will the dream die or will it make it? Will they make it or will they make a fool of themselves? The question that is asked is, "What if the momentum is bigger than me?" The answer is; simple. The momentum is always bigger than the one being caught up in it. But the comforting thing is in knowing that the one who brings the waves of acceleration and the momentum is also bigger than anything that could threaten our lives, dreams and goals.

I am convinced that those who exhibit a level of thrill and comfort in the face of pending momentum are those who have resolved in their hearts to trust God and trust in the bigger picture that they will be ok. Fear of success is a greater pandemic than the fear of failure. It is the biggest type of paralysis that people wrestle with when it comes to pursuing our dreams, goals and visions. It is what keeps us on the shoreside of life and from the pursuit of discipline. It stifles creativity. It stunts growth and learning, and it fosters complacency. The turns, tunnels and curves associated with momentum can intimidate only when there is a complete absence of trust. For the circumstances that are out of your control are only seen as threatening when you feel no one you can trust is in control.

I recall when this surprisingly became real to me. It was right after the air band on flights were lifted after 9/11. For my work, at the time, I travelled coast to coast across my great Country of Canada. In fact, when 9/11 hit, I was on a business trip, and had to take a train ride home from Montreal after being held for two extra days because of the pandemonium. But a few months later, although there was work being done and new efforts to counteract terrorism, work had to resume. And that meant that I had to start flying again.

It was one of those first flights, still relatively early in the fight against terrorism. The fear and the tension everywhere were palpable. From the airport to passengers on the plane. I had resolved, however to trust in the fact that God was in control of my life, as much as I was now out of control. Well, don't you know that was one of the most turbulent flights I had ever experienced in my life up until that point! It was one of those flights where a roller coaster drop of at least two seconds was felt. Two seconds falling in a plane feels like an eternal drop. The shrieks and gasps with every air pocket drop on the plane tore through the tense atmosphere. The clenching of the chair seats and arm rests were obvious as I looked immediately around me. I recall saying a silent prayer. Not a *rite* of passage prayer, to be clear, rather, a *right* to trust prayer. There was such an immense level of peace that filled my heart at that time. It calmed my heart and assured me of my destination. But almost as soon as that peace came to me I heard an outburst from the woman behind me saying; "Let me off this plane, I don't want to die!" It was loud enough for everyone in the two rows behind and ahead to hear. It was a contagious cry and I heard whimpering right afterwards from others around. I don't know what came over me, except the boldness from my prayer, but I turned around and before I knew what to say through the gap between my seat and the seat next to me. The following words came out of my mouth, "You will not die and we will not die because *I am on this plane*! We *will* get to our destination"! Now you have to understand, I did not plan to say that. It was ballsy. My quieter, meeker self was even shocked. But by then, it was already said out loud. She looked at me, and she sat back in her seat and didn't cry out one more time.

When the threat of fear and panic try to overwhelm you in life, that's not the time to stay quiet. Don't let your fear do all the speaking. Speak back to it! It's time to get ballsy! Be bold and be strong about it too. Speak to yourself, to your situation and reaffirm where your trust lies. You will not go down. You will only bypass the attempted derailment to your end goal and achieve unprecedented things. You have a destination and you must resolve that you will get there. Even in the gross darkness of compounded fear around you, both externally or internally, your light of bold confidence can dispel the dark.

Bravery alone is not the absence of fear. Confidence is. Bravery without an underlying confidence can sometimes be dismissed as moronic and ignorant. Bravery that stems from a confident trust has a different feed from ignorance. It is anchored in a solid knowledge that sometimes cannot be explained. It is nestled in the assurance that you have a purpose to fulfill and the Manufacturer of your purpose has a destination and end goal for you to do. Anything short of that is an attempt to derail and sabotage your purpose.

Fear is afraid. The very nature that it projects onto people is the very components of its own character. And so, to feed fear with more fear is to give it life and authorize it's continued expression. As a child, I remember being told by my Grandmother that dogs can sense, even smell fear. It attracts the very thing that you fear. As little children, my cousins and my brother and I were playing in her front yard, when a lose Pitbull from the neighbourhood started charging our way. With every panting growl, we scattered like flies and screamed. Some of us made it into the house but others didn't. My brother was one who didn't make it into the house. From inside my Grandmother's home, while looking through the front door, I witnessed my brother being chased down by that dog. My brother had run up into a near-by tree, but not before being mulled by the dog with his teeth locked into my brother's thigh. Those scars remain to this day. Witnessing fear-based trauma can root itself in your memory and even become dormant if unaddressed. My brother was cared for at a local hospital, and shortly after, he healed up and moved on to continue living his active life as a boy. But that image of that experience was still in my mind. It was not too much longer after that, when our Father bought us a dog. A dog! We never owned a dog before. And this was not a little Chiwowa. It was a breed between a beautiful larger German shepherd and a gorgeous Labrador. The wisdom in what our father did is really only now fully realized in my adulthood. Our father did not want that fear to have power over my brother and I. Well it worked. We fell in love with our beautiful mutt, and we dismantled the smoke and mirrors of fear by calling him Smokey!

Unaddressed, embedded fear-based images in the minds of people is the hook and lure, if you will, for fear to be triggered in multiple instances of our lives. Triggers always happen later than the traumatic incident that instilled the fear. Triggers also are signals that the fear is left unaddressed. The best way to address any fear is to face it full on. If we return to our surfing masters analogy, unaddressed fear is what keeps people on the shores and sidelines of life. It is what paralyses people from moving forward with their goals and prevents them from riding the wave of momentum. Every surfer acknowledges the present reality of sharks and danger; like, sting rays, jelly fish and strong undercurrents. Yet their bravery, most times is anchored in a confidence that is beyond their ability to explain to others. It is usually just observed, not understood. Because the understanding will only come, when others get in the water and face their own fears themselves.

CHAPTER & JOURNAL REFLECTION:

1. Would you say that you are riding the waves of your journey or observing from the shores of life?

2. Name the venture/ventures that you stepped out to achieve or would like to achieve. What are the associated feelings that come when you think of that/ those ventures?

3. Which do you fear; increased momentum or stagnation? Give some thought to your answer and list the reasons why.

4. Have you ever been paralysed by fear? Were there any memory triggers associated to that fear paralysis?

5. How can you address those unresolved embedded fears or images?

Journal your thoughts here:

Charmaine R. Cooper

CHAPTER 6

Review and Refine

Hindsight isn't always twenty/twenty. If it is unattached to a plan of refinement for your future, it can be debilitating. It can flood you with a surge of regret, looking through a lens of the past. Looking at your past experiences, your past passions and your past journey is a part of who you were. But it doesn't necessarily reflect who you are!

A mid-life woman who looks back and sees that her life devoted to her children by being a phenomenal Mother can be nostalgic and filled with gratitude. It can also be discouraging if she may have gone through a divorce and the children are grown and now pursuing their own lives with very little time spent with her. Does the mother see the value that her past experience offers her now or does she only see very little return on her investment? The lens through which she sees her past choices determine the steps she makes for her future.

A young man who reviews the opportunities that came his way from his years of basketball disciplines can be a source of pride and appreciation. But they can also be filled with regret and rejection if he was turned down and not picked up by any basketball scouts who watched scores of his games. Does he blame his coach? Does he blame his parents? Does he blame himself? These are riddling questions that can influence and shape his outlook on life and discipline. How he views the worth of his years spent in training up to that point is significant to how he will be able to move forward with his purpose. Will he see those years as a waste or as a school of learning and development. Will he apply the lessons offered to the choices that he will inevitably have to make for his future? His answers to these questions will not only determine if he will be better over bitter, but they will determine if he will become brilliant!

There are benefits to stepping away from the immediacy of the experiences of our lives and taking a balcony perspective of reflection. Similar to the puzzle pieces of the tables of our lives, those benefits include being able to observe things on a much larger scale instead of the low altitude level of being in the experience. Ronald Heifitz and

Marty Linsky in their book; Leadership on The Line1, called it stepping away from the dance floor. On the dance floor of life, we are too involved to see a bigger perspective. We are too close, too woven into the fabric realities of it. It is not until we step off the dance floor, be-it through the passing of time or distance from the other participating dancers on the floor of life that we can truly see the rhythm, the mapping out of the steps and purpose of the dance. They can see where the crowding was. They can make note of where the ebbs and flows were. They can see where the bottle-necks were and where the momentum was. They can see who were dancing and who were the ones holding up the walls. A balcony view sets one up to access their involvement in the dance and also their former steps. Not only that, but it also offers perspective of where that dancer wants to and needs to go next. What takes place next is just as important, if not more vital than observing from the balcony of the experience. It is getting back onto the dance floor. Planning a course of action is potentially the most critical component of life, not just learning from it.

So many of us leave the dance floor prematurely. Our feet hurt. The music isn't what we wanted, and the dancers are not what we expected. We

---

[1] Heifitz Ronald, Linsky Marty: *Leadership on the Line*. (Boston, Massachusetts: Harvard Business Review Press, 2002).

are disillusioned, disappointed with others and even ourselves. We check out and observe the reel to reel review of our lives as if our best days are behind us. That is the furthest thing from the truth. We must not only review our experiences of the past and learn from them, but we must also refine our mission as a result. We must take stock of our roles and actions in our experiences as well.

A great artist will step away from his/her sculpture or painting to review and then return later on to refine it. It is the combination of *review and refinement* that sharpens the clarity of the purpose of that art piece. In fact, the purpose of the art piece is only a small reflection of the purpose of the artist. That artist gets better and more confident as they get more proficient at the tandem partnership of *review and refinement*. Before you know it, this brings their work before many in museums, auctions and even investors. The Artist becomes more than just an artist, they become a part of the shaping of artistic culture.

It took Michelangelo four years to paint the ceiling of the Sistine Chapel. Using new techniques and difficult procedures, he had to implement constant review and refinement. It is said that the scaffolding was created uniquely for him to allow Mass to still take place below. And that the curvature of the scaffolding matched the curvature of the ceiling. Over time, he developed back injuries and severe vision damage due to the over-extended arching and reaching up that he employed to finish his work. It became apparent that the purpose of this inspiring, iconic art piece was beyond the commission of Pope Julius II at the time. Michelangelo wasn't even a known painter at the time of being commissioned to paint the Sistine Chapel. As a young artist from his twenties to the age of thirty-two he was a sculptor. An iconic sculpture that we know well, is the sculpture of David. This 1501-1504 masterful marble sculpture was made by the brilliant Renaissance artist as commissioned for the Florence Chapel. His accomplishment was widespread, and his reputation, established as sculpture. As so, in light of his past accomplishments and experiences, one can only imagine the amount of self-review and reflections from his sculptures that Michelangelo personally did in order to create another unprecedented cultural icon piece that was outside of his repertoire. His work speaks to generations still today.

Your reputation can precede you and it can also confine you. If you allow your past experiences, opinions from others, criticism and accolades alike to shape you, it can rob you of your destiny. Just because you have never done something before does not remove the possibility of it being done by you. Your qualifications are not limited to your skills and training. Your skills and training are a small reflection of your qualifications. This is a counter-cultural view that is often hard to embrace. Inside of every man and woman lies untapped brilliance and creativity. But that doesn't mean that it must stay untapped. Updated studies have debunked the myth that humans only use ten percent of their brains. We have been told that our entire lives. And when you are told something long enough, it becomes your truth. The truth is humans are using nearly 100% of their brains every day. There are so many elements to human function. And the brain is at the centre of anatomic function, as a result of the brilliance of the nervous system. However, if that where creativity comes from? Is that where Michelangelo found the inspiration and groundbreaking methods to create something never created before? I'm certainly not a Neuroscientist by any stretch, but I am an avid believer in the Creator giving people (His creation) the DNA of His own creative ability. That comes from a different source than the brain that occupies 3-5% of the body's weight. It comes from another source.

Each person can release purpose while they are literally discovering it. It is the creative exchange of reviewing the past to refine your future. Contrary to the popular belief of the messiness of projects, you can allow the mastery to be revealed in the midst of the rubble. You can discover the brilliance even in the immense darkness. As a by-product of the process, you can create unimaginable possibilities that astound even yourself.

Review and refinement are the staples to purpose oriented living. Just because you always did something one way, doesn't mean that you cannot do it another way! Just because the dance floor of your life shows a variety of successes and failures doesn't mean that any life worth living is left on the dance floor. You can start living again. You can start living again now. In fact, the balconies of our lives are as valuable as the dance floors of our lives. If you employ the practice of *review and refinement* often enough, you will most assuredly experience a rewarding rhythm that cannot be ignored and will not be denied. I believe that the litmus test for a lived-out purpose is the ensemble of the preceding principles.

CHAPTER & JOURNAL REFLECTION:

1. When you review elements of your life, are there more feelings of regret or feelings of growth and learnings accompanied with it?

2. What would taking a balcony perspective look like for you in this instance?

3. What can you learn from the balcony perspective of this/these past events that you couldn't learn from the dance floor perspective?

4. Were there other critical participants of your story on the dance floor? What were their roles?

5. What would taking a perspective from the dancefloor reveal to you?

6. Are there elements of your life that you can apply *Review and Refinement* that can impact your outlook on your purpose/goal?

Journal your thoughts here:

The Purpose Project

Charmaine R. Cooper

CHAPTER 7

Embrace Your Purpose

When you try to embrace someone, who does not embrace you back, it is one of the most awkward, mis-fitting feelings that is felt. But when you embrace someone who is as affectionately involved in that embrace as you are, it is one of the most fulfilling of experiences. People embrace people every day. I dare to submit that there are many who have grown all too comfortable with the pursuit of being embraced by someone who will not or cannot embrace you back. The syndrome of loving someone more than they love you has been a part of the human experience as far back as time can trace. Why have unequal and imbalanced pursuits become an acceptable norm in our societies? What is it about the chase in light of rejection that compels us to cling on even more tightly? Somewhere in human reasoning, there is a belief that we are not worth the mutual embrace. That we are not embrace-worthy, if you will. And therefore, compromising ourselves and settling for mediocrity becomes appealing because it is seen as being better than having no one to embrace at all. This is true for embracing things, not just people.

Look around you. We embrace things every day that cannot embrace us back. The pursuit of happiness for many, can be summed up with acquiring all the bells and whistles of life. We embrace faster and nicer cars, money, bigger homes, higher seniority in our careers, and the list goes on. Somehow we believe that embracing these shinier things equals the happiness that we desire. But ask anyone who has lived a while, even has acquired many, if not all of these "items" and if they are truthful with you, you will see that these acquisitions were eventually met with disappointment. These are mere things that are associated with living in a world that promotes them as worthwhile pursuits for happiness, while never delivering on its claim. These acquisitions are set up as things that will qualify you to be classified as having experienced the ideal life meant to be lived. But it is a lie. Because the insatiable pursuit never ends due to the constant push and pull. How is that living? When life is always seen as something to still conquer and achieve, it is never attained. The life you were meant to live is not one that leaves you pursuing for more without end. Rather, it is the one that pursues you back. It is one that embraces you with mutual intent. It is a life of purpose that both presently finds you and is found by you.

A purpose-oriented life pursues and embraces you. It finds you no matter what status of life you may be at, no matter what your past experiences may have been and no matter how much you may have already divested in other empty pursuits.

A young girl who grew up seeing the injustices that her mother underwent in an abusive relationship, finds herself one day later in life, launching and leading an association for battered women in abusive domestic relationships. A young man who was labelled with Attention Deficit Disorder (ADD) in grade school due to not being able to learn the curriculum through traditional methods can also trace back early signs of his purpose pursuing him. He was dismissed as the least likely to succeed due to different learning habits, although the truth was that his IQ was misread, and misinterpreted. Later in life he finds himself creating a platform for creative thinkers and learners around the globe that shake the traditional approach to learning styles.

A quiet and shy child who loves to doodle to express himself and escape a world that he does not understand but observes, later becomes a renowned artist that inspires a new paradigm shift in arts and culture. These all are examples of purpose that is pursuing people throughout their experiences of life. Only when that individual, however recognizes the truth and accepts it, can a mutual embrace take place.

Your purpose will embrace you. It will affirm your place in the world despite the assumptions or classifications of others. It will even affirm you despite your former beliefs about yourself.

To embrace your purpose back, however, you need to let go of the former destructive beliefs that you once embraced. Have you ever tried to "fully" embrace more than one person at the same time? Not quite the same as one full embrace with one person, is it? You cannot embrace multiple people or things all at once. In order to embrace one thing wholly, you must let go of the former thing completely. These supplementing objects of embrace are often cold and disconnecting. They break down who you are as a whole and have you believe who you are only in part by the things that you experienced. For example, someone's abusive part of their life will try to convince them that they are without value. Someone's former sexually exploited living or innumerable indiscretions will try to have them believe that that is all they will ever be: an exploited toy and object or an uncommitted person, incapable of true intimacy. Someone's misfit in early education may have them believe that they are not smart enough and cannot learn new things.

These disconnecting, supplementary objects of thought will not embrace you back, but they will divide you. They will deceive you. The division and deceit are internal. It is often private. It is deep. An approach towards healing is the only way towards mending parts into a whole again.

Forgiveness towards others and towards yourself is an important step towards healing the wounds that continue to gape and disconnect you. Because dividing, supplementary thoughts are private, the needed steps towards healing are often to be public. Exposure of these lies is to be done in the company of others who can be trusted. This may include but is not limited to; A counsellor, a mentor, or a true friend. Exposure to light always dismantles the dark. Letting go of disconnecting empty embraces is a process. But it is not impossible. The amazing thing is, your purpose isn't just awaiting you to get things together. Your purpose is right there in the healing process with you. Right in the fire. It is waiting for you to embrace it back.

The industry that I spent twenty-plus years of my life in started to feel as if it was closing in on me. There was a rhythm, a familiarity and a comfort level that I started to find myself settling into. The learning curve eventually became small and the challenge, minimum. Was this my purpose in life? To be complacent or comfortable at what I was being paid to do? Even though I thoroughly enjoyed my work and had grown exponentially over the years, something seemed like it was missing. I just didn't know what. The change that is needed to propel you to your next layer of purpose always comes at the appointed time. It never comes too early or too late. It is always right on time.

The timing for my change came with a sudden force. I went from functioning efficiently and productively in my role to having my leadership capabilities being questioned and doubted by my direct employer. Over the span of the next three years, I wrestled in a dark space, questioning my own value and worth. Towards the second half of those three years, I started to revisit my purpose. I began to ask myself if I was trying to hold onto something that was not holding me back. I reviewed the desires and dreams of my own life twenty plus years earlier. And I dug my heels in deeply to face a dormant giant that I left unaddressed for years. The incompletion of my formal studies in a field that was completely different than the one that I was currently in, was a twenty plus year old giant that I chose to sweep under the rug. It was a dark time of my life, where I had just lost my Mother and was deemed a failure and drop-out, out of school. It was no longer easier to ignore that dark reality. Because what would have been worse would have been to remain in the darkness of my current reality, ignoring the truth, when purpose was trying to reveal itself to me. It wasn't that I was incompetent in my current job, it was simply that my time was coming to a close. This role that I embraced so much was showing its true hand to me. It was pointing me back to the crossroads of my past, where I left one embrace to embrace another.

And so, I acknowledged a time to change the guards and I chartered a course to greater purpose. In due time, I resigned from my role and recommenced my formal education to complete my Master's degree. I launched myself as a freelance consultant to supplement income (still in my former trade industry), and launched a communications business venture. These are all things that I had not planned to do. If someone were to tell me years earlier that it would become my reality, I would have laughed. But once I embraced my purpose, although I didn't know the details of the plan, I trusted in the One who did. From there, momentum and empowerment followed.

Embrace your purpose. Once you recognize the reality of why you are where you are, no matter how you got there, there is an empowerment that will follow. You do not have to make it happen. Force it to happen. Or even chase it. Empty pursuits are chased. Purpose (that has always been there) is to be embraced. Understanding the difference is significant to a level of peace that you can receive. There is no striving in your purpose. There is only peace. Peace as only God can give.

CHAPTER & JOURNAL REFLECTION:

1. What have you embraced that has not embraced you back?

2. How can you change the narrative around this imbalanced relationship?

3. Was there a disconnecting thought that you were told about yourself in the past that has become a part of your thinking today?

4. What was that disconnecting thought?

5. Was there a truth that you were told that you have now come to believe that you can embrace for healing?

6. What is that truth?

Journal your thoughts:

The Purpose Project

Charmaine R. Cooper

CHAPTER 8

Submit Your Purpose Project

The Project of YOU does not have to be arduous. It does, however, take patience. As we have seen, it takes time, attention to detail and a courageous resolve to discover and embrace. In light of the preceding chapters discussed, I would be remiss to deny the fact that there have been many individuals who have discovered their purposes early in life and have embraced it. But, there are countless scores of people who have failed discover and then submit their purpose.

Let's unpack this a bit further by reviewing our natural projects. When you have gone through the various phases of any project around the home, at work or in formal education, there comes a point where something final has to be done. You cannot fully move on to the next project without doing it. Oh, some have tried, but there always remained a loitering thought in our minds of the incompletion of that task. There is no sense of completion or closure until this final step is done. That is: to submit the project for grading, evaluation or for some sort of response from the audience, partners or authority. There have often been timeline windows associated with these projects that are worked within. Although, it at times can contribute to added pressure, having time lines is a good thing. It helps to serve as a reminder of the project's importance and priority. Without the gentle reminder of time sensitivity and the declining window of grace for that project, the outcome is at the risk of never being completed and submitted. Whether we feel ready or not, these projects, at some point are submitted to professors, boards, employers and even ourselves at some point for a sense of completion.

Can you imagine being thirty years old and never having submitted your seventh-grade science project? What sort of memories would you have had to deal with the years following the seventh grade? What if you neglected to finish the baby's room in anticipation for his or her arrival nine months later? Where would the baby sleep? How unsettling could your night's become, unnecessarily? How about the Summer project initiative that you and your team needed to submit to the board to be considered for roll out the following year? If you never submitted the proposal plan, what would the board be able to use as a base of acceptance or denial? Although it is possible to leave projects un-submitted, it is not possible to have closure without submitting them. Regardless of the outcome or appraisal, a sense of completion comes only after having submitted your project. Although life continues and new opportunities may come, these former and significant opportunities are not just delayed, but they can become lost. Lost opportunities have been the Bain of people's existence since time began. I am referring to the regret and plight of many people over the years. Submitting the project comes in many shapes, sizes and phases of our lives. Submission is often put off because actually letting control go through the process of submission is scary.

The word *submission* has been diced, sliced and criticized. People of all walks of life resist the word because they view it as a threat. In life, there comes a time when we must submit our lives to something or someone beyond or greater than ourselves. Without denial, every human being must come to these cross roads, in their various forms, sooner or later. What people choose to do in light of these cross roads often vary, but they come.

Contrary to the highly controversial view, matrimony is about mutual submission. Marriage is about two lives that come together with intent to complement and enhance one another. But what is often not spoken about is the intrinsic surrender that is entailed in the vows that are exchanged. It is a sort of submitting to the concept of complete acceptance of one another through thick or thin, good or bad and even until death. For the rest of their lives together, couples who wed are saying that they are open to feedback, growth and yes, evaluation. Now, already to many people, the word *evaluation* sounds so negative and confirms for them why marriages should be avoided all together. The question must be asked, "When you commit and submit one life to another, is that essentially what you are doing? Submitting yourself to evaluation?" The answer is yes and no! Let's spin that perspective on its head. When someone commits and submits to another person, they are not submitting to future *pending* evaluation but rather to former completed evaluation. In other words; acceptance! They are embracing the fact that they have already been completely accepted based, even chosen on levels from a former evaluation, and therefore the evaluation existing between them is not contingent upon performance but based on established approval. The true sense of acceptance that every human being craves only thrives in close relationship. It is a proximal evaluation not a distal one. Close relationship is essential for healthy and trustworthy growth to take place. It is also necessary for submission of one's self.

The idea of submitting your life, your dreams, your very purpose for existing

is a conscious and vulnerable one. With everything in our past, both failures and successes, there comes a point where we must recognize that there is a window of time afforded to us to reach an internal resolve. A resolution is the understanding that we have already been accepted by God! This acceptance is independent of what we have done. It cannot survive or be attached to any action or status. It is solely based upon the worth of who we are. We have been created with purpose because we are filled with DNA of purpose. It is an intrinsic acceptance not an extrinsic one. This is what makes it so challenging for performance-based individuals to receive this form of acceptance. It therefore makes it extremely difficult to release one's performance-based life for submission.

Yes, there are those who submit their lives and purpose early in life. But the reality is many people wait until their latter-years of life before submitting their final project of themselves. Some wait until their last breath. We see it every day in hospices or the winter of the lives of many people. The Priest or Reverend is called in for rites of passages or the overdue private talk. One can only imagine what happens in those final moments of life. Speaking from the experience of watching my Mother die, I recall the days leading up to her death and how they were filled with an overwhelming desire to make things right with the few people that she had fallen out with years before. I loved and still do love my Mother. She was one of the most giving, selfless and godly women that I knew. But she wasn't perfect. For the sake of this point, I will explore why my Mother did not make it right with those individuals before she became sick? She was adamant to make it right with them on her dying bed. But why not when she had ample opportunity? Firstly, for obvious reasons, she wasn't aware of the window of time closing on her life. No one is. Secondly, when she was healthy, she claimed more control, than really was her own. Like the right to be in control. The right to view her unwavering position as being right. Even though, those few broken relationships indicate that brokenness was present. I asked myself, how could it be possible for a woman who submitted the majority of her life to God, still left unsubmitted areas of resentment and bitterness until days before her death? I think that not only of herself, but I must now gage my own actions and choices based on the same question posed to myself. It may not be in the form of bitterness or exactly how my Mother experienced it, but have I submitted my purpose, my goals, and my life completely? Or am I still waiting for when the elements of life line up?

Multitudes of people go to their graves having never submitted their final project. Submitting their heart. Submitting their disappointments. They won't submit the *project of themselves*! The good news is that if you are reading this book, there is still time. The window is closed only when we draw our last breath. Therein lies the paradox of both the beauty and the heartbreak of this reality. Submission is a conscious but vulnerable one. You submit to acceptance and you give up the striving for control. The submitting of yourself is only willingly done when there is a trust in something or someone beyond yourself. That is when you can let the reigns go.

CHAPTER AND JOURNAL REFLECTION:

1. Do you feel that you are losing something of great value when you submit to something or someone else?

2. If yes, list those things that you feel you are losing.

3. What does the word submission mean to you? Describe your feeling?

4. Do you feel you can achieve more being accountable to only yourself, rather than being accountable to someone else or others?

5. What are the dreams, goals, visions of your life that you are still holding onto too tightly?

6. What are the held onto opinions, perspectives and viewpoints that you feel could be hindering your complete submission?

Journal your thoughts here:

The Purpose Project

The Purpose Project

CHAPTER 9

Re-Connect to Rest

For many people, it is common practice, after a long work week, taxing school semester or major project for people to get away for the weekend, get by the water or take a vacation? This is often referred to as reconnecting. There is an underlined thought that if one needs to reconnect, it is likely that they endured a period of feeling disconnected while in project or work mode. But what is it exactly, that they felt disconnected from? What is it about the water, social companionship or the mountain-eques landscape that pulls people to want to feel reconnected? It has to be more than just the water itself, but rather the rhythm and roar of the crashing of the waves along the shore that speaks more deeply than water on its own. It must be more than the beautiful landscapes of nature's most beautiful mountain expanses of the world. But rather the awesomeness of their existence and the creative enormity that surpasses human understanding. Surely it is also more than just getting together with some good friends that you could get together with anytime. But rather the desire for heartfelt engagement and companionship.

Intrinsic in every person is a desire for connection. But is it to be connected to nature and people or are those only elements of a yearning for a deeper and different connection?

Vacations end, weekends eventually wrap up in preparation for the next world week and people can disappoint us just as we can disappoint others. This yearning must be for more.

When we owned Smokey, my German Shepherd/Labrador dog, we loved him immensely. We adopted him as an older pup and he affectionately grew up with us as we grew from children to teenagers. He was a great source of joy, exercise and also worry. You see, Smokey grew up on a farm where he was breezed with his siblings. And although he did not grow up on the farm or with his siblings, there were natural bents and behaviours that he demonstrated that were not suited for the suburban life.

When he got to a certain age as an adult dog, something fascinating started to happen. Every end of week, like clockwork, Smokey would dig a ditch in our backyard under our fence and take off onto the soccer field to run up and down as fast as he could. Sometimes there were even soccer games going on when he did this. My Dad repaired that whole under the fence countless times, but the born retriever and explorer in Smokey found a way to break free and "reconnect" to something that was calling him without fail. As he grew older, he would disappear for more than a few hours. It started to grow to a day then even up to two days. We always went looking for him. Sometimes we found him. Sometimes we didn't. Even though he would always return, this is where it started to truly concern us. What was happening? Why did Smokey start to display these actions that he hadn't ever displayed before. It was only later that we realized that Smokey wasn't doing anything out of nature to his natural purpose. To connect the explorer that he was to the free uncaged expanse if nature around him. We were caging him in. Even though we loved him.

When we desire expression, communication and reconnection. It is only because of our internal purpose to reconnect to the Creator of us all and rest from the toil of life. Being alive does not have to include the feeling of endless toil. And although I am an advocate for financial success, finances are not the determining factor for the cessation from toil in life. You can work and still be engaged in life without being caged in life. But that only comes from giving your life the reconnection it craves. It's reconnection with God.

God is not a made-up idea to pacify ignorant people. God is not a concept that is intangible. God is not an entity far away from earth looking at mankind from a distance. God is relational and relevant to every aspect of life.

His voice can be heard more than most people think. Not in the typical way. But in plentiful ways. You can hear Him in the crashing of the water waves on the shores. You can hear His whispers through the trees of the forest and see His majesty in the breathtaking mountains. You can also connect to elements of Him through other people. These are the reasons where our hearts crave these surroundings. And like an exploring dog, your heart pulls you towards what is calling you the most. It's a call to rest. It's a call to reconnect. It's a call that can be answered at any time.

Our beloved Smokey never did find the farm country grounds that his nature so desperately tried to find. He was eventually hit by a car as he also started to exhibit signs of dementia. Smokey must have spent the last five years of his life digging holes under our fence and taking off on his explorations. One day when he hadn't returned for two plus days and we couldn't find him

We knew something was severely wrong. The next day a stranger came to our door and said that they found him a couple of miles away hit by the side of the road. We were heartbroken. But if I were to be honest, I was also relieved. He was finally at rest. And what our caged love could not provide for him, was now closed forever.

We are not called to live lives similar to that of k-nines. And I am certainly not advocating that we are of the same class. But I do believe we can take stock of our lives and pay attention to life lessons all around us.

People can cease from toil and enter into true test, when we reconnect to our source of companionship, our source of purpose and our source of fulfillment. As we submit our lives to the one who loved us before we even entered the world, we can enter into a confidence of fulfilled purpose. No matter what stage or level that we may find ourselves in life.

For it is only the originator of purpose is the one who we find fulfillment of purpose in. He is not only the giver of life but relationship with Him is the fulfillment of life!

CHAPTER AND JOURNAL REFLECTION:

1. Where do you find the most reconnecting places in your life?

2. Do you feel more disconnected or connected most of the time?

3. What is it that you feel calls you the most? What is it about that thing, person or place that is so appealing?

4. Now take it a layer deeper. Is there more behind that thing, person or place that you ultimately need to connect with?

5. If you think so, how will you make that connection? Is it important to you to do so?

Journal your thoughts here:

The Purpose Project

CONCLUSION

The Purpose Project is the most important project that you will ever find yourself either ignoring or embracing, because the Purpose Project is only revealed through you. The level of importance that you place on this project determines so much of our interpretation of the various phases and stages of our lives. Choosing to ignore the one thing that is used to fulfill your existence is a price that is far too great to pay. Some recognize that early, while other recognize it late in life, if at all.

What about you? Now that you, likely have counted the cost, examined what it will require and even acknowledged some of the derailing distractions, there is a choice to be made. And don't fall for the lie of not making a choice. For to put off choosing, is in itself a choice that remains with us every day that we are alive.

Make the choice. Choose to see the adventure of this project for what it is. A journey of growth and expansion. Embrace the manufacturer's guide and go ahead; complete and submit the project. For if you will, I think you will be surprised to see that the grade that has already been given to you, is one that has already been marked GOOD.

THE END

RESOURCES

Heifitz Ronald, Linsky Marty: *Leadership on the Line*. (Boston, Massachusetts: Harvard business Review Press, 2002).

Manufactured by Amazon.ca
Bolton, ON